SURVIVING

DESERTED ISLANDS

Samantha Bell and
Heather Kissock

MEDIA ENHANCED BOOKS
AV2 BY WEIGL
ADDED VALUE • AUDIO VISUAL
www.av2books.com

Published by AV² by Weigl
350 5th Avenue, 59th Floor
New York, NY 10118
Website: www.av2books.com

Library of Congress Cataloging-in-Publication Data
Names: Bell, Samantha, author.
Title: Deserted islands / Samantha Bell.
Description: New York, NY : AV2 by Weigl, 2019. | Series: Surviving | Includes index. | Audience: Grade 4 to 6.
Identifiers: LCCN 2018053484 (print) | LCCN 2018054314 (ebook) | ISBN 9781489697790 (Multi User ebook) | ISBN 9781489697806 (Single User ebook) | ISBN 9781489697776 (hardcover : alk. paper) | ISBN 9781489697783 (softcover : alk. paper)
Subjects: LCSH: Islands--Juvenile literature. | Wilderness survival--Juvenile literature.
Classification: LCC GB471 (ebook) | LCC GB471 .B45 2019 (print) | DDC 613.6/909142--dc23
LC record available at https://lccn.loc.gov/2018053484

Printed in the United States of America in Brainerd, Minnesota
1 2 3 4 5 6 7 8 9 0 22 21 20 19 18

122018
120118

Project Coordinator: Heather Kissock   Designer: Ana María Vidal

Every reasonable effort has been made to trace ownership and to obtain permission to reprint copyright material. The publishers would be pleased to have any errors or omissions brought to their attention so that they may be corrected in subsequent printings.

Weigl acknowledges Getty Images, Alamy, iStock, Shutterstock, and Dreamstime as its primary image suppliers for this title.

First published by The Child's World in 2016.

DESERTED ISLANDS

Contents

Chapter 1

Storms can disable boats by pushing them onto large rocks.

A Very Long Wait

In the early 1800s, the Nicoleno Native Americans lived on San Nicolas Island near California. But hunters moved in to catch sea otters and seals. The hunters fought with the Nicoleno. Many members of the group had died by 1814.

Some people wanted to help the Nicoleno by getting them off the island. Captain Charles Hubbard and his crew arrived in 1835. He was going to move the last people off the island. Fewer than 12 Nicoleno were left. They boarded the ship. But one of the mothers realized her child was missing. She begged to go back. The crew let her search for her child. But they left while she was gone. A storm likely caused them to leave in a hurry.

People tried to find the woman. But no one could. Then, in 1853, Captain George Nidever sailed to the island to hunt. He found the lost woman. She had not found her child. She had survived alone on the island for 18 years.

The woman was scraping blubber from a piece of sealskin when Nidever found her. She smiled and spoke in a language Nidever did not understand. Her clothes were made of animal skins.

The woman was happy to see the rescuers. She went with them back to California. Nidever and his wife brought the woman into their home. They named her Juana Maria. Juana Maria enjoyed seeing all of the new things in the town. But she was also eating different foods. Her new diet and surroundings caused her to become sick. She died just seven weeks later.

Blubber

Blubber is a thick layer of fat under some marine animals' skin. It helps store energy and keeps the animals warm. It also helps them float. Animal blubber is also good for people. Some people who live in cold climates use the blubber as food. It is a good source of vitamins C and D. Vitamin C helps heal wounds. Vitamin D helps build strong bones. People long ago also used blubber to make soap.

People have become stranded on islands throughout history. Some people have been left behind, like Juana Maria. Others have been **shipwrecked**. Getting trapped on a deserted island is rare. It is especially rare today. People have better ways of traveling and communicating than in the past. But no matter how people end up on a deserted island, it takes a lot of hard work to survive.

Juana Maria hunted seals on the island. She ate their blubber to survive.

The **Nicoleno** are believed to have lived on San Nicolas Island for at least **8,000** years.

The 1960 novel ***Island of the Blue Dolphins***, by Scott O'Dell, is **based** on the story of **Juana Maria**.

Sealskin is **water-resistant**. Native Americans used it to make **boots**, **tents**, and **boats**.

Chapter 2

Staying warm is a top priority in colder climates. Survivors must stay dry in order to stay healthy.

Survival Needs

Islands can have many different types of terrain. Some have cliffs. Others have sandy beaches. Islands in colder areas can have a lot of snow and ice. But **castaways** all have the same basic needs no matter what the island is like.

People must drink water to survive even if they do not have food. You can live for weeks without food. But you can only live a few days without water.

Castaways can melt snow or ice to get water in cold areas. Place ice in a tin can or other container. Then, set it near a fire. You can lose body heat warming it with your body. On warmer islands, there are more ways to get fresh water. There may be small rivers, springs, and streams. You can look for places where the plants are green and healthy. This means there is water nearby.

Survivors may find plastic containers onshore. They can use these to store fresh water.

Some islands have sandy shores. Here, you can dig until you reach moist sand. Water will gather in the hole. The salt water will sink to the bottom. It is heavier than fresh water. Then, you can drink the water on top.

Large rocks on shore often have small pools of water on them. But you cannot drink from them. The pools will be salt water. They are made when waves hit the rocks.

Survivors can collect water to save it. Seashells, coconut shells, and even shoes can hold rainwater. You might also find things washed up on the beach that can hold water. Joseph Rangel and two other men were stranded on an island off the coast of California in October 2000. They had gone the wrong way during a fishing trip. Strong winds ran their boat aground. The island was rocky and dry. The men could not find any fresh water. But they did find four bottles of water and a can of soda that had washed up.

You can drink from a coconut if there is no fresh water. Coconut water is a clear liquid in the center of young, green coconuts. It is full of good minerals such as **potassium**. Potassium helps the body's cells, tissues, and organs function. Brown coconuts contain coconut milk. A large one may hold as much as one quart (0.9 liters) of milk.

Shelter is also important for survivors. It can help even in warm weather. A shelter can be as simple as a place out of the wind. A cave can make a good shelter. Or you might find an old building to use if people have lived on the island before.

Collecting Water from the Ground

It is possible to collect water from the ground with a solar still. To build one, dig a large hole and place a container in the center. Cover the hole with a sheet of plastic. Hold down the edges with rocks or sand. Place a small rock in the middle of the plastic so it sags. The Sun heats the air and soil in the hole. The water evaporates. It hits the plastic and turns into beads of water. These run down the plastic into the container.

Coconut trees require warm conditions for successful growth. This is why they are typically found in the tropics.

Sometimes, castaways have to build a shelter. You will want to find a place near fresh water. You can build a simple shelter using plants. Find or cut two long poles into a Y shape. Stick them in the ground. Lay branches and leaves between them to form a roof. This can protect you from rain.

Island castaways can often find plants and animals to eat from both the land and the ocean.

Many kinds of seaweed are safe to eat. Seaweed is a major part of people's diets in some parts of the world. Some seaweeds can be dried and used for months.

Mollusks, such as mussels, clams, and sea snails, are also safe to eat. The best time to look for them is at low **tide**. You can look in rock pools or dig in the sand. Worms and insects are options, too.

In 1921, 23-year-old Ada Blackjack joined a group of explorers on Wrangel Island in the arctic. Their ship got caught in the ice. Some people left to get help. Ada stayed behind to care for a sick man. The man died. She was left alone for four months. She ate eggs, birds, and seals to stay alive.

Mussels often group together in pools or on logs and rocks.

Chapter 3

The shape of a teepee fire allows oxygen into the fire to feed the flame.

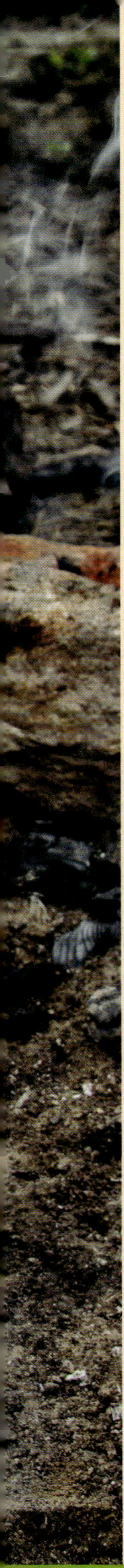

Island Activities

You might imagine living on an island would be like a vacation. But people trapped on deserted islands must work hard to survive.

Survivors will want to build a fire even if they are in a warm place. Fire keeps people warm. But it can also be used to cook, boil water, and dry clothes. Fire can keep insects and animals away. It can also be used to signal for rescue.

You can build a fire with tinder, **kindling**, and logs. Tinder is anything that will light quickly. Dead grasses or leaves make good tinder. It can even be a strip of cloth or some pocket lint. Once the tinder is burning, add the kindling. Then, add larger pieces of wood to keep the fire going.

One of the best ways to make a fire is to build a teepee fire. Just like the name, the kindling is arranged in the shape of a teepee. The tinder is placed in the center and lit. Logs are added as the fire grows. Teepee fires provide the most heat and light. They are also resistant to snow and rain. Because of the shape of the fire, sparks and smoke tend to go straight up. This can help rescuers notice them.

You might not have matches to start a fire. Try using a magnifying glass, camera lens, or broken bottle. Move the glass so that the sunlight focuses on the tinder. You can also use **flint** and a steel blade to start a flame. Strike the flint with the blade to make hot sparks. Make sure the sparks fall on the tinder.

Survivors should keep their fire going all the time. If there is not much wood, you can light it only when it is needed. Otherwise, keep the fire going. That way you do not have to relight it. Use large branches to keep it going. Push them into the fire as they burn.

The Moon and the Tides

Tides are the rise and fall of ocean water. The sea comes far up on the shore when the tide is high. The water moves back out at low tide. The tides are caused by the gravitational pulls of the Moon and Sun. The Moon's pull is stronger because it is closer. The water moves to high tide when the Moon is closest to the ocean. It also swells on the opposite side of Earth. In between are low tides. The tides go in and out as our planet rotates.

While an island may have a lot of useful things, there are often dangers as well. Many islands have coral reefs nearby. Coral is sharp and can cause painful cuts. Some kinds of coral sting.

Barracudas have been swimming in Earth's oceans for approximately 50 million years.

Many fish that swim in the reefs are poisonous. Eating one of these fish can cause numbness, itching, nausea, or worse. Avoid eating any fish unless you know it will not hurt you. Some species are even dangerous to touch. Toadfish and stonefish have venomous spines.

Jellyfish have stinging **tentacles**. Sea urchins, anemones, and sponges can cause painful injuries. Some reef fish give off electric shocks.

Castaways must also watch out for animals that bite. Sharks, barracuda, moray eels, and sea snakes will bite if bothered. Crocodiles live in saltwater bays and can swim in the open sea. Females guarding their nests are especially dangerous. Ada Blackjack had to look out for polar bears in the arctic. She used a gun to scare them away.

Survivors on the beach should watch for changes in the tide. Look for the farthest line of weeds and shells that have washed ashore. This tells you how far the water reaches. Be sure there is higher ground to go to when the tide comes in.

Beware of strong currents if you go into the water. When a beach drops off suddenly into deep water, there will be a strong **undertow**. Tie a safety line from you to a strong tree if you go in.

Castaways on a deserted island must always be on the lookout for rescuers. But seeing them is not enough. Survivors must also be able to get their attention, sometimes from far away.

A **stonefish** can survive up to **24 hours** out of water.

Saltwater crocodiles can grow to more than **20 feet** (6 meters) in length.

A **jellyfish** can **sting** even after it **has died**.

Fire is one way to signal rescuers. Build a large fire on the highest point on shore. You can make a lot of smoke by burning damp or green wood.

When someone goes missing at sea, rescuers use helicopters and airplanes to search for them.

Reflected light also attracts rescuers. Look around on the island for anything that will reflect the Sun. You do not need a mirror. Any flat, shiny surface will work. Even people signaling with shiny credit cards have been rescued.

Survivors should also be ready if a plane flies overhead. You can arrange rocks or other objects to attract attention from above. In April 2014, five snorkelers became stranded. Their boat drifted away with all of their supplies. They were stuck on a tiny island near Australia. The group used rocks to make a giant SOS in the sand. This signal means that someone is in trouble. A rescue helicopter saw their message after nine hours.

People have been stranded on all kinds of islands. Some were alone, and others were in groups. But with the right knowledge and a no-quit attitude, castaways can survive long enough to be rescued.

Timeline

People have become stranded on deserted islands under a variety of circumstances and over long periods of time. While many have lost their lives waiting for rescue, others have survived and made it back to civilization.

1541 Banished to a remote Atlantic island for breaking ship rules, Marguerite de la Rocque survived for several years before being rescued.

1704 After arguing with his ship's captain, Alexander Selkirk asked to be left on an uninhabited island near Chile. He was rescued four years later.

1723 When the pirates who had captured him went ashore for water, Philip Ashton escaped into the Roatan jungle. He survived there for 16 months before being found by English woodcutters.

1841 Manjiro Nakahama and three friends were fishing off the coast of Japan when a storm arose. The teenagers were shipwrecked on Tori Shima Island for almost six months before being rescued by a passing American whaling ship.

1914 On an expedition to Antarctica, Ernest Shackleton and his crew became stranded when their ship became stuck in ice. They made their way to nearby Elephant Island, where they set up camp. Shackleton was able to eventually reach a whaling station, where he organized his crew's rescue.

2004 A deadly **tsunami** hit Indonesia on Boxing Day, sweeping many people out to sea. One Indigenous woman, known only by the name Jessy, was able to escape the tsunami's wrath by running inland. She was found 45 days later on the island of Pillopanja, where she had survived on coconut milk and jackfruits.

Island Watch

Islands are scattered throughout the world. Some are large, while others are tiny. Keeping track of happenings on these islands can be challenging. Collaboration between various search-and-rescue groups is common.

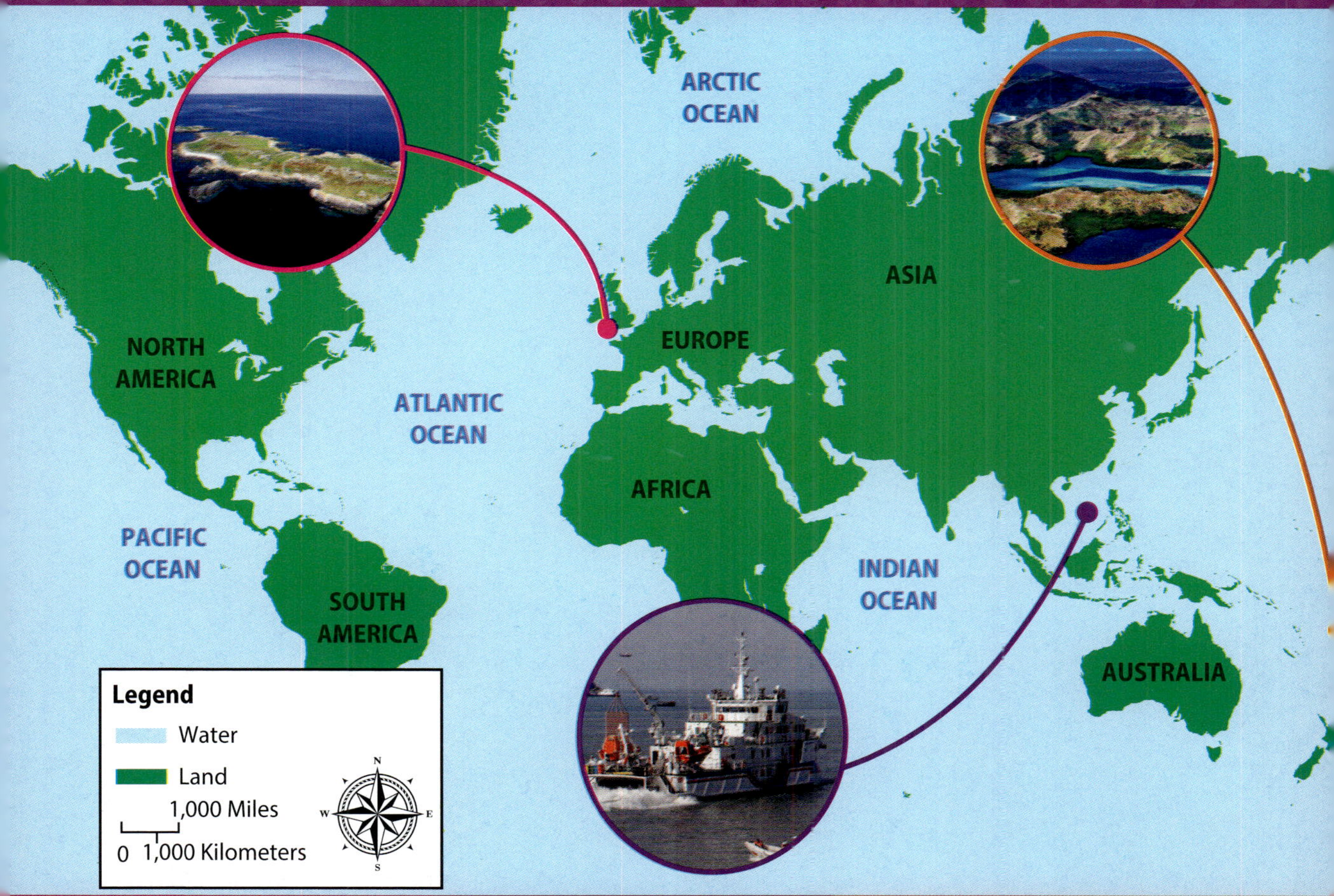

Channel Islands Air Rescue Channel Islands is a helicopter-based service that operates in the English Channel. It acts as both an air ambulance and a search-and-rescue vehicle.

China In 2018, China sent one of its maritime search-and-rescue vessels to be permanently stationed on Subi Reef Island. This is the first Chinese ship to be assigned to this type of role.

Fiji The Pacific Search and Rescue Steering Committee is a collective of nations that conduct search and rescue operations in the islands of the Pacific Ocean. Fiji became a committee member in 2017.

Quiz

1 What book is based on the story of Juana Maria?

2 What mineral does coconut water contain?

3 Where was Ernest Shackleton heading to when his ship became stuck?

4 What can be built to collect water from the ground?

5 When is the best time to look for mollusks?

6 What causes tides?

7 How does the shape of a teepee fire impact its sparks and smoke?

8 What part of a toadfish is venomous?

ANSWERS **1.** *Island of the Blue Dolphins* **2.** Potassium **3.** Antarctica **4.** A solar still **5.** At low tide **6.** The gravitational pulls of the Moon and Sun **7.** It sends the sparks and smoke straight up. **8.** Spines

Key Words

castaways: people who are cast adrift or ashore, usually far from help. People shipwrecked on an island are castaways.

flint: a hard, dark rock. Flint and steel can be used to create a spark.

kindling: small sticks or other materials that burn easily. Survivors must have kindling to start a fire.

mollusks: a group of invertebrate animals with a soft body and usually a hard outer shell. Many people like to eat mollusks.

potassium: a mineral that builds proteins and muscles. Coconut water contains a lot of potassium.

shipwrecked: when a boat is destroyed or lost. Boats can be shipwrecked when they hit rocks or reefs.

tentacles: long, flexible limbs. Jellyfish have stinging tentacles to help them catch food.

tide: the rising and falling of the surface of the ocean. The sea comes up on land the farthest during high tide.

tsunami: a large, destructive wave. Tsunamis are caused by earthquakes.

undertow: the current beneath the surface of the water that moves away from the shore. Undertow can pull swimmers out into the ocean.

Index

Log on to www.av2books.com

AV^2 by Weigl brings you media enhanced books that support active learning. Go to www.av2books.com, and enter the special code found on page 2 of this book. You will gain access to enriched and enhanced content that supplements and complements this book. Content includes video, audio, weblinks, quizzes, a slide show, and activities.

AV^2 Online Navigation

AV^2 was built to bridge the gap between print and digital. We encourage you to tell us what you like and what you want to see in the future.

Sign up to be an AV^2 Ambassador at www.av2books.com/ambassador.